Simple Revolutionary Acts

To Dave —
Who Loves you!
ME!

Simple Revolutionary Acts

✦

Ideas to revitalize yourself and your workplace

Todd Conklin, Ph.D

iUniverse, Inc.

New York Lincoln Shanghai

Simple Revolutionary Acts
Ideas to revitalize yourself and your workplace

iUniverse, Inc.

For information address:
iUniverse, Inc.
2021 Pine Lake Road, Suite 100
Lincoln, NE 68512
www.iuniverse.com

ISBN: 0-595-32065-1

Printed in the United States of America

Contents

Section One: Revolutionize The Way You Think and Feel About Your Work

Section Two: Revolutionize How You Interact With Others

Section Three: Revolutionize What You Do

Foreword

o o o o o o o o o o o o o o o o o o o o o o o o o o o o o o o o o o o

"All revolutions are impossible until they happen, then they are inevitable."

—*Albie Sachs*

Once in a great while, a workplace will get lucky and have a very special person on staff. This special person may be a leader, a friend, a mentor, or a co-worker. While the person's title hardly matters, the impression this special person makes on the other workers within that organization is important and meaningful. This person has great ideas and moves with a certain amount of spontaneity throughout the workday. This person makes working fun. This person has the ability to make what we do—day in and day out—a little bit more exciting, a little bit more fulfilling, and more fun.

Chances are, if you are not one of these special people, you are very interested in making work more meaningful for you and your workplace friends. That is great! Don't be afraid to try new things or to break up old patterns of behaviors, individual or collective, that exists where you work. Boldly try these simple revolutionary acts.

Perhaps you fancy yourself as one of these special people. People who consciously strive to make their work a little better are the people who would pick up this book. Welcome to this information. Add, subtract, change, tweak, move, fold, spindle, or mutilate this information all you want. Just make a promise to yourself and your co-workers that you will try every day to build a more satisfying workplace.

It would be great if we could revolutionize our jobs and create positive changes in our workplaces, take the time to awaken the fun part about doing work, shake up some of the old habits we have all gotten ourselves into. All we need do is decide that we can personally revolt against the way our workplaces are now. We can make a difference! Then we can perform little subversive acts that make big differences in the way we treat one another in our workplaces. Good revolutionary acts come in small packages.

Now, let's go start a revolution.

Simple Revolutionary Acts

○ ○

"Make bold moves, knowing that some will work and some won't.
Or make no moves, which guarantees that you'll be an also-ran."

—Steve Chaddick, Sr.V.P., Ciena Company

Introduction

I hope you love your job.

It is possible to love your job. There are people who love their jobs. You may even know some of these people. It often makes me wonder what secrets these people know about work that the rest of us do not know about our work? Believe it or not, this secret is more about how these people feel and respond to their workplaces. Love for one's job is a pretty good indicator that your workplace is a creative and stimulating environment and, therefore, a pretty good place to spend the majority of your waking hours.

But, these workplaces are rare. Sadly, many people do not love their jobs. People who are having difficulty loving their jobs cannot find a sense of belonging in their work environment. Work is often seen as a form of punishment, not a form of reward. Many go to their jobs and work without ever feeling a sense of excitement, fulfillment, and satisfaction. Most managers all want to have "a workplace of choice," unfortunately, countless workplaces fall short of that mark.

People who do not feel they are employed in a workplace of choice may act as if they are a group of zombies with jobs. I know this because one day I realized I did not love my job. I had become bored with my work. Life seems to be passing so quickly, and I was losing valuable time doing things that did not seem important to me or to the world around me. Somehow, I had settled for a work environment I did not like, want, or desire—or had ever imagined for myself. I had fallen into the most common form of complacency: I had lost sight of the fact that work should be fun, rewarding, and satisfying. All I had was a job.

As a result, I felt burned out, tired, under-utilized, poorly managed, under-appreciated, cheated, poorly compensated, stressed, scared. These feelings simply begin the list of any of the thousands of other reasons that force us to see work as an obligation rather than opportunity for growth.

I began to ask myself, "Why do so many people find themselves in a working-zombie state?" "Why do normal people settle for workplaces that are far from satisfying?"

Fear of job security, national security, workplace stability, economics, and what the world may present us with next can cause workers to feel at a loss. Social and political events in the world around us may force workers to believe that they must learn to survive in an environment that does not offer satisfaction but that does offer job security and a paycheck. It is a difficult and scary time to be at work. Keeping a job is important; in fact, it seems at times that keeping a job may be more important than being happy and fulfilled in a job. These are tough times, but deciding to be happy should not be a tough decision. Workers seem to have developed an idea that can be summarized like this: "I must have money; therefore, I have to work. Happiness, I assume, will come later." The problem is, many times, happiness never shows up.

Think about a few questions: Should we accept the fact that our workplaces are becoming less fulfilling and much more impersonal? Is it good to let work become more efficient and less fun? Should we lie down and let our companies use our bodies as machines? Must we be exposed to one more idiotic management policy that is not based on a legitimate business reason or need, but on the bureaucratic result of some person's insecurities in their position in our workplace? The answer is no. We need to direct change both in our lives and in the parts of our workplaces that we control. We must make our world better and different, not faster and cheaper. We must do it for our own sanity. What we need is a change, a revolution.

You have heard it before, and the adage seems to stay true: The only constant in the workplace is change. Certainly, the way we do work has already changed. There's e-mail, voice mail, and interoffice mail; call waiting and call forwarding; the paperless office, the remote office, "hoteling," and even the office-less office; downsizing, right sizing, outsourcing, second sourcing, and re-sourcing. There's the Internet, the Ethernet, the local net, teleconferencing, telecommuting, and plain old telephoning. There are literally zillions of ways we can interact or connect with each other in this age of communication. Yet, we may be losing the one most effective, most important form of connecting with each other. We have forgotten how the way we interact person-to-person is important to our happiness and sense of meaning at work. The form or way that we choose to communicate with each other has an impact on the message and the intentions that we send and receive. We have forgotten how much better face-to-face conversation is when compared to a demand or a flaming e-mail or just plain mean-spirited communication with other people.

There are many of us in the same situation of feeling disconnected, without reason, passion or calling, and this feeling is probably much more normal than it is abnormal. We have somehow "normalized" our poor work environment and jobs without meaning as a part of our regular workplace expectation. We have become comfortable and complacent. Sadly, we are waiting for something to change…when in fact; nothing will change if we do not change it for ourselves.

Working

"The one thing that worries me is the possibility that we will create a world that is much more economically efficient, but that is much less satisfying to live in."

—*Thomas Malone, Sloan School of Management*

Many changes in the workplace have a lot to do with improving the bottom line and little to do with improving human relationships or the quality of our work lives. Improvements are happening, but they have proven to be less than ideal. Instant communication, the global network, forming partnerships with people you never met, electronic meetings have become part of our everyday reality. We were promised that technology would allow us to do our jobs more efficiently without ever leaving our comfy chairs and without ever having to have a face-to-face conversation. An unintended consequence of this increased efficiency presents us with a workplace that technically is a more efficient place to work but socially is much less satisfying.

Revolutionary thinking is a great way to change the world. Some revolutions are bloody. Some are bloodless. Some revolutions are for excellent reasons. Others are ego-driven travesties. Regardless of motivation or outcome, the key to all revolutions is to change the way the world appears to those who live in it. We—peers, workers, customers, and partners—need to assume responsibility and change our workplace environments. We must ensure work is meaningful and enjoyable, while at the same time efficient, profitable, and effective. We must learn that we have much control over our own workplace destinies. Furthermore, because we are working in the problem, we need to work from within our workplaces in order to attempt the solutions. The revolution must begin from within.

Start Simple, Stay Simple

"Life is not measured by the number of breaths we take, but by the moments that take our breath away."

—*George Carlin*

It would be great if we could revolutionize our jobs and make some positive changes in our workplaces, take the time to awaken the fun part about doing work, shake up some of the old habits we have all gotten ourselves into. It would be great if we could perform little acts that made big differences in the way we treated one another in our workplaces. Good revolutionary acts can come in small packages. I am not suggesting acts that cost thousands of dollars and lots of effort and time on anyone's part, but, sure, we all want to come into the office one day and tell the entire staff to pack a bag and put the newspaper on hold for two weeks because we're going to some fabulous resort to ski, swim, and get in touch with our "inner account manager." Simple little acts that help people see the workplace and themselves differently. We cannot wait for the miraculous. Instead, we can start small with actions that change the way we think about our workplaces and ourselves. These acts are quick, cheap, and easy to do—and you do not have to pack an overnight bag or send your dog to the kennel.

The Acts

"Here is a test to see if your mission in life is over: If you are alive it isn't."

—*Richard Bach, Illusions*

What every good workplace revolutionary needs is a list of some simple revolutionary acts to use in the workplace to start the process of re-energizing the human relationships that are the very core of workplace happiness and satisfaction. What follows is a single list of simple revolutionary acts that is divided into three sections.

- The first section of this list of revolutionary acts addresses the importance of changing the way you think about your workplace.

- The middle section of this list addresses the way you communicate within your workplace in order to help produce change.

- The final section of this list of revolutionary acts is made up of some suggestions you may try in your workplace.

These are just suggestions, not some type of brilliant list made up by famous management gurus. Use this list to jostle your mind into creating your own list. You know your workplace. You know your co-workers, staff, peers, partners, clients, and customers. You know what may or may not work for your environment. All you have to do is pick one or two of these simple revolutionary acts and try them. Collect your own data. See what works for you.

Section One:

Revolutionize The Way You Think and Feel About Your Work

Always choose the positive solution

When given two options, always pick the answer that is most positive. Learn to lead every argument by saying, "Yes." Teach yourself and the people around you to begin most encounters with a yes. Yes may not be the right answer, but it starts every workplace meeting moving in a forward direction. Both choices may lead you to the same conclusion. If the choice you make is the wrong one, who cares? The next time you make a decision, you will have learned from the last decision you made. Work is like that. Work is an accumulation of many decisions you have made, but work never allows you to get to the end of that accumulation. You never get to the grand total of work. You only get to this moment. Why not choose the positive solution? Even though you may not end up at a yes answer, you have started this process with a forward-moving push. It is easier to stop a yes at some point midway through an encounter than it is to start a yes after all momentum is lost.

Be Kind

How can kindness serve as an act of revolution? Try this sociological experiment in the next couple days. Consciously try to build the self-esteem of every person you encounter for an entire day. Do this by being as kind as you can in every circumstance of your life for this day. Observe your behavior to see how you feel about yourself and others and how your time is spent during this period. See if simply being kind is effective. My guess is that you will see and experience a marked difference in the quality of this day. Perhaps kindness will be the most important revolutionary act of all times. What seems to matter and what is most obviously is missing from so many of our workplaces can be summed up in one simple but profoundly strong word: kindness. Many people have lost track of how important it is to be kind to one another. Co-workers are not kind to co-workers. Customers are not kind to front-line people. Bosses are not kind to workers. Workers are not kind to bosses. This is a tragedy. Being forced to spend time in a place where people do not understand nor practice the art of being kind is horrible. Stand up and stop this kindness drought. Demand that you treat all people with kindness. Hold people accountable to be kind to each other by reward kindness when you see it and questioning unkindness to you but more importantly to others. Consciously model kindness to the people who are around you. Consciously (meaning on purpose) attempt to be as kind as you can be to every person you encounter. It all boils down to this: The real payoff at work is interacting with each other in a way that leaves us feeling better about ourselves and about each other. The one way to effectively maintain our self-esteems is to simply be kind to each other. It is not weak, wimpy, or less than professional to be smart and kind, strong and kind, wise and kind. However, if you aren't smart, strong, or wise remember the most important of all is to be kind.

Be the person you've always wanted to be

It is never too late to become the person you always wanted to be. So much about who we are in the workplace happens without knowing that we have *choices* about who we are in the workplace. Self-concepts are by definition the way that we conceive of ourselves, what we think about ourselves. The way you perceive yourself also dramatically changes how other people perceive you. Our internal conversations have tremendous power in forming the way we see our workplaces and ourselves. Organizations that build special identity cultures spend a lot of time, effort, and money in getting their workers to think in ways that produce higher levels of production. Much of this "thought control/identity control" is done entirely to make the work more efficient for the company, not for the individual worker. Many of us have been trained in the habits of highly effective workers. This type of training does exactly what it promises it will do. This training causes workers to evaluate their internal conversations in order to be more effective workers. This simple revolutionary act, the act of being the person you always wanted to be, asks you and the workers around you to become more highly effective people who happen to be at work. In many ways, being the person you want to be may be the ultimate form of workplace revolution. Be the person you want to be at work, not the person the workplace wants you to be. Try this technique as a starting point. Go to work thinking good thoughts about the day that lies ahead. The attitude you don on the way to work makes a difference in the way you will perceive your day. That simple difference in perception will become amplified and become a better working environment. Try it; the best data I can ever give you is an example of how well this simple revolutionary act works in a real workplace.

Choose Happy

Happiness is an important goal to have as you begin to reinvigorate your workplace. In many ways, how you respond at work is as simple as knowing that when people are given the opportunity to choose their emotional responses—and human beings always have the opportunity to choose, they can choose a response that produces happiness in themselves and the people around them. Working with people who are happy would be a big difference to many of us. How can we help ourselves and other people in our workplaces choose happy as an emotional response? You pick how you respond to people and situations in your life, period. That is it. You are in charge of your feelings and responses. I do not say these things to be sharp, harsh, preachy, or judgmental. This idea can be a difficult concept to understand and one that many of us forget. The profound truth is that you chose your attitude; no one else can do it for you. When you realize this powerful fact you will have learned the most important coping and strategy tool that is available to you. This may sound a bit oversimplified. Choosing happy is an ongoing challenge. We must understand that much of the way we react to everyday workplace situations is based on the way we choose to feel. Perhaps the most revolutionary decision you can make is to let yourself react to situations in a way that is positive and forward-moving for you and your workplace. We are not our jobs. We are people who work very hard at doing our jobs. By simply choosing to make our workplace relationships happy, we have already revolutionized our thinking and therefore changed the environment in which we work. Try practicing this skill. Try choosing to approach life's situations from a position of happiness. If you have never consciously tried choosing happy, you are going to surprised by what a difference it makes in your life.

Be Courageous

I once worked with a fireman who explained one of the most important skills he had developed over his years of responding to emergencies was the art of pretending. This big, strong rescuer had learned that if you do not *feel* brave, you *act* brave; if you don't know what to do, you act like you know what your doing and you go do it. If you believe you can do it, chances are you will do it. It takes guts to change you. It takes even more guts to change your workplace. Pretend, every day, you are the bravest, smartest, richest, and wisest person in the world. Eventually, you will become the very person you are pretending to be. Practice the act of being courageous around issues that have relatively low consequences. Learn how it feels to take a risk and win and how it feels to take a risk and lose. As you become more comfortable, you will find your courage creeping into the bigger, more important, parts of your life. Be brave. Be bold. And then be ready to pretend to be brave and bold even when you do not feel brave and bold.

Decide what you want, then make your plan

Think about where you want to end up, and make your plan moving backward from that point. This technique may not give you a complete plan, but it will position your thinking and the thinking of your work group in a way that is much more encompassing of your real workplace. Think tactically as well as strategically. Countless stories can be told about folks who had a great plan and for some reason managed to mess it up by not starting this great plan with the right foot or not bringing on the right people or not presenting the right information to the right crowd at the right time. Think about where you want to be, what you want your life to look like, how you want your workplace to look, smell, or feel, and then build your plan around that end target. Think about this goal before you start the journey. Then think about what you should being doing today to get to this end point. The clarity and direction this tactic will offer you is worth its weight in gold.

Be a bit ornery

Be a bit ornery, but make sure to be ornery in the most professional way possible. I like people who see the world a bit differently than I see the world. I like people who have a bit of an edge on them. These little bits of personality make the workplace a bit more exciting. Irreverence, a healthy lack of respect, and being brave enough to break a rule are all good qualities in a worker when these qualities are pointing toward making the workplace more meaningful and fun. Breaking the rules often is the only way to realize how ridiculous the rules are. Some rules need to be bent and twisted a bit just to see what happens.

Take yourself, and those around you, less seriously

Let's face it: If you really look at your workplace you will find a bunch of pretty stupid stuff going on. What we think is so important, so end of the world, is often a simple flash in the pan. The world is a huge place, and we are but one little-tiny part of that giant world. Our workplaces have traditionally rewarded avoidance behavior because we learn that if you avoid a problem long enough, almost all problems eventually go away. Most policies are not very thoughtful. Most rules exist to serve people other than the people doing the work or getting the service. Questioning authority more often leads to a positive answer than to any negative consequences. All of these policies, rules, and bosses are either tragic figures or parameters around our work—or they are just plain silly. I would always choose to laugh when allowed the luxury of response. Laugh at work. The sound of laughter is the same sound that new ideas make when they are being born. Be willing to laugh with your co-workers, with your customers, even at yourself. More importantly, create a working environment where laughter is allowed as an appropriate and even positive contribution. With a 100% guarantee, you can be assured funny things happen to you at work, and they happen more often than not. Enjoy the ability to immerse yourself in the ridiculousness of your work. If you can't laugh at what is happening in your workplace, the menu of attitudes and choices for how you feel about work all become somewhat depressing. Be aware of times when laughter really will be the best medicine, and then administer the proper dosage to the people around you. If you feel sad yourself, try to remember why you are doing these simple revolutionary acts. When bad things happen, and they do all the time in the workplace, we need to simply back up a couple of steps and look for what is funny. There is always something funny.

Many times, there are multiple things that are funny. Find the funny parts of work and hold on to them as coping mechanisms. Many times, the funny parts of work are the only parts that keep us coming back.

Make sure you are self-sufficient

No person is an island. We all need each other much more then we realize. Yet, in today's workplace, you probably should be a fairly strong peninsula. It is important to be able to provide your own support. It makes a difference to know your own way around your computer. You really should be able to identify when you are feeling a bit burned out by the system. Find things you like to do that rejuvenate. Leverage your discretionary time to do work projects that you find interesting. Always be learning new skills, having new ideas, and looking for ways to revitalize your own career. Think ahead. Have a goal. Be your own counsel and advisor, but be willing to listen to others. Be your own quality assurance inspection, but be open to new and better ways to do your job. Be in charge of your own workplace happiness, but never turn down the chance to let another person make you happy. Always have a current résumé. Part of being self-sufficient is knowing you have much control over the way people perceive you and you have much control over how you leave an encounter. When I do anything I always think about how I will begin an encounter and how I will get away from the encounter. Always think about an introductory and exit strategy. When I go to a party I plan some type of entrance and exit strategy before I ever walk in to the room. You never miss a chance to manage an impression.

Revolutionize How You Interact With Others

Everything in your workplace happens through conversation. Really, Everything

The more I become interested in how to revolutionize our workplaces, the more I realize how important the simple act of talking to one another is in making changes happen. Everything we do happens through conversation. You are constantly modeling behavior, changing viewpoints, convincing non-believers, inventing new ideas, and moving mountains by simply having conversations with those people who are around you. By knowing that conversations are the only way that we successfully accomplish our lives, we begin to realize how important it is to talk about the work you are doing and the environment that you are doing work in. This same idea holds true about the way you want work to happen and the satisfaction and meaning you want to extract from this work. We are always adding and subtracting from our workplace by talking about what we do. Taking the time to have a conversation is not only how we interface with one another, it is also the only way to change in your work environment.

*Perceive more about the world
and the people you are working
with than these people perceive
about you*

As simple revolutionary acts go, the act of out-perceiving the people around you has long-term positive consequences for the happiness of those around you and, of course, for yourself. In many ways we, as workers, don't pay attention to the millions and millions of signals being sent to us every day. If you do pay attention, you know that a very small amount of information is actually ever given to you verbally. Most of the indicators of how a conversation is going are non-verbal. These forms of body language play a very important role in your method of perceiving information about your workplace. Knowing (or accurately guessing) what may happen next is a form of reading the organization's non-verbal or non-espoused communication. You have many ways to gather information about your workplace. Use this information to strategize what will happen next. It works. You will immediately notice a couple of things. You will notice that you are right much more than you are wrong in guessing the potential changes, impacts, and directions in your workplace. You will also notice that by having a better understanding of what is currently going on, you will also have a much improved understanding of what may happen next. Knowing what may happen next is often the most important piece of information you can have. That knowledge gives you freedom, control, and a form of security about your work situation and the people around you.

Reactions are meaningful—monitor them

I think of reactions as being meaningful in much the same way I think of the difference in meaning between the words "reaction" and "response." Follow either of those words with the phrase "to medication" and you will begin to get a much clearer understanding of the effect these words have on coloring our response to workplace events and situations. When people react to medication, it is usually considered to be a bad thing. When people respond to medication, it is usually considered to be a good thing. When people react around you, something is happening that you should pay attention to. People who are reacting to a situation are clearly telling you how this situation is affecting them. When a person is upset, most likely this person is trying to make sense of the world around him or her. Don't underestimate the comments or emotions around a person's reaction to some event that is taking place around him or her. People who have a reaction to events in your workplace are trying to figure out what is going on, which is why these people react the way they do. If a person reacts strongly, the person is trying to make sense with the same level of intensity as the level of their reaction. If a person takes something that has been said as personal, that comment was somehow personal to that person. There is much you can observe about your workplace by simply monitoring your peers, friends, partners, customers, and co-workers for their reactions. The part of this revolutionary act that is important is the observance of these reactions in order to determine how you should respond. Your response matters greatly. Work at moving your response to people reacting to the world around them from one of "how a person affects me" to "how is this person reacting to the world around him or her?" When you try to understand people's reactions to the world, think of the story of the fellow driving up a winding mountain road. Just as he turns around a bend in the road, he meets a red convertible sports car driving in and out of his lane at a high rate of speed. The man is surprised and looks at the driver as the sports car passes. The driver of this sports car looks at the man and yells the word "Pig!" right at him. Our driver, continuing up this mountain road is suddenly offended, hurt, angry, and upset. He has been so taken by the rudeness and brashness of the other driver that he resolves to turn around and follow that little red car, to confront the other driver about this behavior. As our driver slows to turn around, he is shocked to see—standing in the middle of the road—a pig. Had he not slowed down, in a sense heeding indirectly the warning given him by the other driver, he surely would have hit this animal. Reactions and responses count.

Help people realize work is not fair

I work with large groups of people, and I am constantly amazed at the resilience and power that people have in their workplaces. People speak freely about the methods they have adopted to cope with favoritism, ineptitude, and inequality. Yet, within the group of people I call my co-workers, I see a much different picture. Work is not fair. Some people get better treatment than others. As difficult as it is to stomach, it is very powerful to realize that work is not fair and it is up to us to decide how we will respond to that fact. It is powerful and freeing to know that, by not having an expectation of fairness, we are never disappointed when events don't go our way. Is it lowering our standards, rolling over, and letting "them" win? Perhaps a person could think that. I submit that knowing work is not fair is more like a secret weapon. It becomes difficult for you to react in a way that may hurt you if you simply do not allow the situation to get to you. Remember, it is only work, and work is sometimes not fair.

If you respond to every situation like an emergency, what will you do in a real emergency?

Hardly any situation is an emergency, unless you are a fireman or a zookeeper. Yet we have this belief that everything must happen this very minute. Even if no one tells us our work is timely, we are so over-saturated by things happening fast that we tend to invent a sense of urgency that may have never been present in the original work assignment. The sense of speed and urgency present in our workplaces is unnecessary and, in many cases, has not been requested by our bosses or customers. We often are given signals that make us think all work is due immediately. In most cases, that sense of urgency is a value we put on the work as workers, not something management has placed on the work. Take time to think about your responses to problems and situations to ensure that you are responding to the situation in a thoughtful way. Reflect not only on how you plan on responding to whatever situation is "shoved" before you, but also reflect on why you're responding the way you're responding. Without sounding too much like an ancient mountaintop sage, I would invite you to pause before you respond to problems. Wait for the drama to settle, think through the pallet of choices before you, and select an appropriate action. Counting to ten when you're angry, never interrupting a person during an argument, and metaphorically looking at situations from 10,000 feet are all very effective ways of giving yourself some time to receive the information, draft a positive response, and then communicate that response or action to the right people in the right way at the right time. The Emperor and philosopher Marcus Aurelius said, "If you are distressed by anything external, the pain is not due to the thing itself but to your own estimate of it, and this you have the power to revoke at any moment."

Your boss is just your boss

Help people understand the boss is just a person trying to make the work go as easily, effectively, and profitably as he or she can. Your boss is not your parent. Your boss is not your high school principle. Talking to your boss should not scare you or make you hold back information or even give you a nervous feeling in the pit of your stomach. In fact, if you are reacting to your boss as if you are in some type of trouble with your parents, you are reacting inappropriately to the situation. Do everything you can to know that your boss, most likely, wants you to respond in more of a collegial way and less as if you were being sent to a disciplinarian. Not every boss is a good boss or even a good person, but chances are high that your boss is doing everything he or she can to keep the train on the track and to please the people above him or her. Most bosses want to be liked, and they want you to succeed and those are the important ingredients to a successful workplace recipe. If your boss is a good leader, then he or she has hired people with personality, talent and skills. Know that you can actively work on how you see and respond to your boss. If you can change the way talking to your boss makes you feel, then you can change the quality and effectiveness of the information you give to and receive from your management.

Reward good behavior, ignore bad behavior

People, like dogs, are pretty easy to train. That sounds a bit pompous and shallow, but like raising puppies, the rules are pretty simple.

The basic principles for human behavior are:

- People will do what they are rewarded to do.
- People will not do what they are punished for doing.
- Reward and punishment are not as clearly defined as you may think. Monitor responses carefully, always.

It is the execution of these simple rules that makes life difficult. People will do what they are rewarded for and will not do what they are not rewarded for. This is the most basic rule of all human behavior, the first principle of getting along with your peers: You should reward behavior you would like to see repeated and ignore the behavior you would not like to see repeated. Your workplace is a lot like a great big sociological Petrie dish: People who are interested in reinvigorating the workplace know that experimentation is a good way to gather data. Boldly experiment with your environment. Try rewarding good behavior and ignoring bad behavior for a couple of days and see what kind of simple revolutionary acts this "behavioral training program" produces in your workplace.

Always remember that people change in small steps

When confronted with an attitude or belief you think is wrong—whatever that attitude is: racism, classism, depression, or stupidity—remember that changes in attitudes or beliefs happen in small increments, and these changes happen almost entirely by conversations. "All or nothing" thinking gets you most often to the "nothing" part of the equation. We move in small steps. Long journeys have many stops. You can't eat a whole elephant in one sitting. You must eat an elephant one bite at a time. Everything that happens in your workplace life probably happened pretty gradually—even if, at the time, it seemed to happen all at once. Changing your workplace will also happen in many small, almost unnoticeable, steps. Your boss moves in small steps. Your friends move in small steps. Your customers move in small steps. Monitor improvement by looking for the subtlest changes in your bosses' or co-workers' attitudes, beliefs, and actions.

Don't ask "Why me?"

Understanding work satisfaction comes when workers no longer ask, "Why is this happening to me?" Helping your co-workers move away from a victim mentality will revolutionize your workplace. It can be difficult, at times, to not think the universe is selecting you as a target and then proceeding to dump all of the trouble in the world on top of you. Everyone has a day or two when they wonder, "What else could go wrong?" Help those around you to disengage from work. You are not your job. Help people remember that hardly anyone has ever died from missing a deadline, few people have been given lashings for having a typo on an important document, and being late for a meeting does not mean you will be thrown in prison. In a way, it's like driving to work in the morning: Some people drive their car like they are taking their child to the emergency room. Other people drive like they are going to work. It's just a job, and the job isn't happening to you as a person, it's happening to you as a worker. Try to remember that asking why events are happening to you is, in a very real way, becoming a victim of your job. You are in control of your job; your job is not in control of you.

Love your enemies

Hmm…think you have heard this before? Yes, you have heard this before, and you should hear it again and again. There is nothing gained from being angry with another member of your workplace. Nothing is gained, but much stands to be lost. Every moment you spend being upset—about being treated unfairly, not being heard, not being respected, feeling cheated, feeling under-appreciated, or whatever has disappointed you—is a moment that you have lost from your life forever. You will never get that moment back. Sorry to be so dramatic, but forgiving your enemies is such a profound way to regain control of your workplace that it simply cannot be understated. When someone does something bad to you at work, do two things:

1. Learn from the experience and protect yourself from something like it happening again.

2. Forgive the whole experience and move on.

Sometimes loving your enemies is a difficult thing to do, but not allowing this situation control over your life is always the best thing to do.

Remember, adults get scared too

There probably aren't monsters in the supply closet. It is a pretty good bet that you are safe and sound where you work. But sometimes monsters are the least of your worries when you are concerned that funding may be cut and you will not have a job. Monsters in the supply cabinet are manageable compared to funding plans and budget forecasting. Work in your actions and interactions with your peers, co-workers, partners, and staff to build a sense of safety and stability when you speak of people's talents, work quality, and careers. Know that nothing will improve—not production, not processes, not operations, not quotas, not deadlines—when the people you work with are scared or feeling insecure. I believe that the sense of job security is the most basic need we have as workers in our workplaces. Without the sense of stability and security from our work environments, nothing else really happens. We are so busy being afraid that we don't build or maintain relationships, we pay no extra care or attention to our work, and we are left with no real sense of meaning or accomplishment. Fear is an amazingly powerful force and, sadly, it is highly prevalent in our workplaces. Think about the times when you have been required to live your life in fear of some type of action or reaction. These times truly are paralyzing and have a very negative effect upon your ability to interact with the other people in you life. Drive fear as far away as you can from your encounters with the other people in your workplace. Do this by always building an honest sense of personal and professional security. Communicate openly and honestly about factors that may have a direct effect upon the future of your organization. When you don't know what the future will bring, say that you don't know what the future will bring. With honest communication and awareness of the security and stability needs of your work group, you really can control the amount of fear in your work environment. Drive this sense of fear as low as you can with facts and honest communication, then sit back and watch the revolution take place.

Care about the parts of people that aren't the work parts

Most management books tell you not to get too involved in the lives of your employees and co-workers, and for many reasons that is probably a safe statement. It can be risky becoming too intertwined with a fellow worker. However, by not getting to know the non-work part of the people you work with, you are missing out on an important part of their lives. Don't pry, don't be nosey, and don't force information from your peers, co-workers, customers, partners, and staff. Simply pay attention to what these people tell you about their lives. This type paying attention to what people tell you about their lives could be called "social situational awareness." You can be effective in being socially situationally aware knowing that when you take care of the people parts of your job first, the process parts of your job work much better. Your workmates will set the line as to how far they want you to come into their lives. In the same fashion, your workmates may also let you in on some very exciting and important parts of their lives. Your responsibility is to pay attention and remember what is being said. Then, engage that information in order to allow your associates to realize that you know how full and important their lives are to them and that you are supportive and interested.

Make time to think about things

For some reason, taking time to think has become a luxury in our workplaces. I can not imagine what could be more important then taking some time to get our thoughts together before we take action or make decisions. I would guess this lack of time to reflect is coupled with the sense of urgency that seems to have overtaken our workplaces. We are in a hurry. We have much to do. Taking time to reflect has been relegated to the back seat. If you make time to reflect you can be assured your work—your ideas, actions, relationships, and responses—will directly benefit from this time well spent. Put time on your calendar to do nothing but think. Make quiet time to reflect on what is happening in your work life. Hold on to that time like it is an important meeting with your biggest, most powerful customer. Don't let this time "slip" on your calendar. Don't waste this time. Make it a regular weekly appointment with yourself—and keep it. You need time to reflect on your world. Take that time and reflect about your work environment. Take time and plan your career. Take time to understand and improve your relationships with people in your life. Try giving this time at least as much importance your schedule as the time you spend forecasting budgets or making staffing plans. Without doubt, people find that taking time to "just think a while" often proves to be a turning point in their most profound personal and professional decisions. Reflecting on your workplace world gives you more power and control over your environment. Taking time to think is the difference between you acting upon your work or having your work act upon you.

Speak the truth

Granted, it might appear a bit dangerous—and there is the risk it could be—but wouldn't the workplace be a better place if people just tried being honest. The act of having all people telling the truth is extraordinary. It is so easy to *not* tell the truth to the people you work with. Telling the truth makes for difficult conversations, and we generally try to shy away from difficult conversations with our co-workers, peers, friends, and customers. But, in many cases, not telling a person in our workplace the truth simply delays the inevitable: Eventually we will have to have honest conversations with these people. We are constrained from honesty by many things. Sometimes it is too risky to be honest. Sometimes it would be professional suicide to be honest. Sometimes honesty is neither desired nor requested from our workplaces. Sadly, some have allowed themselves to believe that not being honest is being cunning and smart. Wouldn't it be nice if we could simply be true to who we are and what we believe? Being honest does not mean being rude or disrespectful. It does mean being truly authentic with the people around you. Remember this adage, "If you always tell the truth, you will never have to remember which lies you told to which people."

Greet people in a meaningful way

I worked for a manager who bounced between happy and stressed-out fairly often. That type of mood swing in many workplaces is pretty understandable. However, when this boss bottomed-out, the behavior that he exhibited when entering the workplace each morning changed quite dramatically. The normal routine for this supervisor was to walk down the hallways greeting each person most every day. If the mood was right, when you went to this person's office doorway you were welcomed inside. However, when this boss was at high-stress levels his tendency was to almost completely shutout the outside world and live entirely in his head. Not greeting people and not welcoming people at the doorway to his office. On these particular days, the staff obviously tended to respond much differently to this boss, what was interesting was that they would also respond much differently to each other. Never let it be said that the way you communicate doesn't matter. It does matter. The way this boss communicated made a measurable difference to the entire environment of the workplace. I learned much from that manager. Perhaps the easiest simple revolutionary act is allowing people to see—in your presence, posture, and language—that you are happy to see them when they enter your workplace. Look them in the eye, smile, and sincerely greet people when you meet them in your workplace. A meaningful greeting provides a positive springboard to effective communication and will produce an immediately difference in the attitude or approach other people take when they come in to your office and meet with you. Make people feel welcome when they come to see you. When people feel welcome they tend to act nicer, laugh easier, and are more willing to move forward to a positive solution to a problem.

Listen to the person talking until that person is done speaking

This simple revolutionary act is easy. Shut up and listen to what people are saying to you. Don't be afraid of a little silence in your life. You will not believe what an enormous difference this one little action, this exercise in personal discipline, will have on the overall quality of your communication with other people. You know by this point in your career that listening is important. You know that listening effectively is hard work. To be truly successful in listening to people you will have to learn that silence is not a bad thing. Don't be afraid to offer some periods of silence during you interactions with other people. Allow silence to happen and you will see that people will find the need to offer more insight and information in to your conversation. Try really listening. Don't fill every quiet moment in business meetings with noise...leave little moments of silence...and see what happens. Little moments of silence allow us to think about what is being said. We have time to reflect upon what was said to us and respond in a way that is more thoughtful. More thoughtful is good. Don't listen to ambush. Listen until the person talking to you is finished. You will be pleasantly surprised by the difference it makes.

Meet new people

Why not take the opportunity to meet some new people? Meeting new people is one of the best ways to revitalize your work life. Find people, who by their presence in your life will allow you to learn new things, have new experiences, think in new ways, and see your work environment from a new perspective. The best way to learn about different ways of thinking is to have a friend who thinks in a new way. I have a friend who is a successful attorney and is painfully shy. He once told me that every time he goes to a professional function, he makes it his goal to meet three people he does not know. He can leave the function only after he meets and has a conversation of with three other people. He does not think of his three-person goal as punishment. Rather, he thinks of it as a form of professional development. Next time you are in a big work crowd, be a revolutionary. No matter what else happens, your personal network will be much larger in no time at all. Best of all, people will know you and you will know them.

Talk to someone
who does not like you

…and then go straight to the dentist for drilling without anesthesia. Hold on. Step back and think why this may be an important revolutionary act. This is a stretch goal for you and for the people who work around you. This is not fun or easy, but it is important to try to build bridges to people who appear to not care for you or your ideas, knowledge, wisdom, skill, or input. Talking to a person whom you perceive may not like you immediately offers you some very important skill-building opportunities. You must rehearse your approach to that person. You need to think about what topic you will try to discuss. Being given the opportunity to rethink your strategic approach to meeting a person who is not immediately aligned to liking you allows for the opportunity to rethink your introduction strategies. You will be forced to look at yourself and those around you in a completely different light. You may not solve whatever problem is holding that person away from you, and that is fine because building a relationship with this person is not the goal. The goal is to create an environment where you can have a polite and businesslike conversation with this person. In attempting that goal, the bonus learning you gather along the way is valuable to you and also to your ability to change the way you see work.

Challenge wrong assumptions, politely

Someone makes a racist comment in your office. What do you do? Every cell in your body is probably telling you to pretend the comment didn't happen. You know the comment was made; now you have the opportunity to make a difference. You don't have to be a hero. You don't have to be rude. You don't even have to try to change the mind of the person who has the faulty assumption. All you have to do is politely disagree with the assumption just enough to get the person with the wrong assumption to stop and notice what assumption was stated. Slowly and surely, as the dialogue around the water cooler begins, your peers, friends, partners, customers, and co-workers will begin to realize that some assumptions these people hold about other people, other cultures, other workplaces, and other ideas may be wrong. Everything that happens happens through conversation. Change always happens by small conversations between people. A conversation about challenged assumptions is the best conversation that can be held because this type of conversation begins the process of changing the way people see their world. Change happens at the most basic levels of human existence, when basic beliefs are expanded. The only way to expand a person's basic beliefs is to have conversations about the ideas that surround and have made up those beliefs. It is nearly impossible to change an assumption a person holds as a basic belief by forcing a person to change. It is almost always possible to change basic beliefs by having a conversation about why they exist.

Appreciate problem solving

Do not think about why something will not work; on the contrary, try to focus on why something will work. If you are really interested in building consensus, try doing it from a positive position in your meetings and conversations. Learn to appreciate workplace situations, not to solve workplace problems. Traditionally, in our workplaces, the way we view problem solving has been through a scientific-method lens. We tend to identify the problem, think of a potential solution, test that solution, and then if all seems to be working, use that solution over and over again. There is absolutely nothing wrong with using this traditional problem-solving approach when faced with issues and situations in our workplaces. However, if you are truly interested in revitalizing your work environment, you ought to know that this traditional approach tends to set all problems, and therefore the attitude workers take in solving those problems, in a negative frame, "problems are problems." There is another way to frame problems. Instead of looking for what needs to be fixed in all situations, search for methods, ideas, and examples of what has worked well in the past and recreate the environment to repeat that experience. Making for a more "problems as opportunities to engage past experiences of success." Focus on the strengths and positive experience that exists within the people who have been tasked to create solutions. Once you have identified these success factors, you have only to repeat them in order to find your solution. All of this is called the process of "Appreciative Inquiry." I invite you to study this idea in more depth.

Ask people to help you solve problems

Asking for help in solving a problem is a very powerful tool. One of the most immediate ways to rejuvenate and revive your workplace is to engage the people around you in a meaningful way to solve problems that exist within your work environment. Asking people to help you solve a problem makes a lot of sense from the knowledge-sharing, idea-farming point of view. Shared problem solving makes even more sense when you consider that you are bringing others into problem-solving activities in order to leverage their specific knowledge, skill, and abilities. This process also engages others by increasing their self-esteem and feeling of being valued. When a worker is invested and involved in the quest for a solution, the problem not only gets solved, but also is often solved more effectively. You don't only get a good answer; you also get an invested population. You may very well be the first person to ever have asked some of your peers, partners, co-workers, and customers to contribute an opinion or idea that will make the workplace better. Try this simple revolutionary act. You will be amazed by how a simple request for help, allowing a glimpse into your inner-humanity, will not only get you a better relationship with people in your workplace, it may also get you the best answer.

Have and express new ideas

View the world differently. Solve problems creatively. Think of new ways to use old processes. Invent something amazing. Build a better mousetrap. We all have new ideas. What we often don't have is the permission to speak these ideas out loud, to give our ideas voice. The revolutionary acts here are twofold. First, we need to have and to honor our new ideas. Second, we have to have the stamina and courage to speak these ideas out loud. Our ideas could be rejected. We could put ourselves in a situation were we could be thought of as silly or stupid. We could also have the idea that actually changes the very texture of our workplaces. Proposing a new idea is definitely high-risk behavior, but if you have an idea that you believe actually "has legs," the real question becomes, "what is there to lose?" That said, how revolutionary is it to create an environment in which ideas can be freely expressed and valued in your workplace? When you truly know the importance of presenting a new idea, you can use this knowledge to profoundly change your work environment by working to create an environment that makes room for other people's new ideas.

Give credit where credit is due

There is nothing more powerful than being recognized for doing good work, and there are few things better than having the reputation for being the person who recognizes good workers. Plenty of organizations have some type of immediate worker-recognition programs. These programs give small awards in order to reward, and thus continue, effective and positive behavior. These programs are great, but knowing how and when to give credit where credit is due is a bit different. Knowing how to stop, look a fellow worker in the eye, and sincerely tell that person that you are glad they are doing the work they do is very powerful and extremely rare. Surprisingly, this simple act is about as revolutionary as any act you can try in your workplace. Noticing a job well done and commenting to the people doing the job you are glad they do such good work is powerful. Making certain you freely acknowledge people who have done work well or made work better or more meaningful is revitalizing to your workplace and rewarding to the workers who did the work. In other words, giving sincere credit where credit is due is a force multiplier and a morale builder, sort of a workplace domino chain of good acts. The key is to "freely" acknowledge these efforts. This isn't about the boss. This isn't about strategically getting people to like or accept you. This is about recognizing little pockets of excellence that exist around you all day, everyday. This is about the work everyone does to get the job done.

Help people around you understand that work is frustrating and ridiculous, and it is not their fault

Its true, your workplace is frustrating and ridiculous—but what is even more profound is that it's not your fault. Our workplaces have stupid rules, policies, processes, and restrictions that are forced upon us and held as the gospel for doing work. Let me share with you the definition a judge would use if asked to determine if a rule is a rule. A rule must have four characteristics: A rule must be written down somewhere. A rule must be communicated to people in some method. A rule must be understood. Finally, a rule must be systematically enforced. Why rules that have no real bearing on our work exist is a big enough topic for a very long conversation, but we know that, over time, rules that once made sense no longer hold much weight to the way we do work. Knowing that stupid work rules are, well, stupid is important in understanding the difference between a real, thoughtful, and meaningful rule and something that someone made up and called a rule. Rules are a good example of why work is frustrating and ridiculous, but we could have just as easily talked about policies, procedures, work instructions, handbooks, and seating charts. You can't change the way work gets managed before it gets to you, but you can change the way you feel about that work. Changing the way you feel about work is your most important tool. One warning, however: This doesn't mean you can go around your workplace constantly lamenting how frustrating and ridiculous work is. No one likes a complainer, even if he or she is correct.

Section Three:

Revolutionize
What You Do

Manage your bosses—aggressively

Or better yet, manage your boss's expectations of your behaviors, performance, and worldview. You have much power over the way your supervisor leads you in your workplace. Use that power to your advantage and set the expectations for how you want to be treated and how you want to be managed. Your boss is trying as hard as you are to figure out your supervision needs. Help them by rewarding and discussing behaviors you want repeated. If you want to start leaving early to cook a meal for your spouse one night a week, perhaps you should present this idea as if it were an idea that was borne of a comment that your boss once made. Give feedback where feedback is due. Give feedback where feedback counts the most. Let your boss know by your behavior, performance, and actions in the work environment how you want to be managed. Then consistently reward that behavior. Try this revolutionary act in small doses with your boss, and you will be amazed at how well this idea works. You have much control over the way you are managed. The trick is to use that control to make your workplace into an environment that best meets your needs.

Gently remind people that we can all be replaced

This isn't meant as a threat. Being replaced should never be taken as a threat to your personal job security. In a way, knowing that you can be replaced is a sign of maturity and good mental health. As hard as it may be to believe, if you make yourself irreplaceable, you will never have an opportunity to grow within your workplace. Having a job that has a logical, next person in line to take your position after you leave is good thing. I would not want to be in a job where I could not be replaced and I certainly don't want anyone working for me that cannot be replaced. You really want to share information, procedures, methods, tricks, and ideas about how you do your work with everyone who works around you. Be a mentor to new workers knowing that you are helping them understand their work and you are helping yourself have the freedom to grow and move around at your workplace. Most importantly, work on convincing yourself that other people can and will do your job as well as you do your job. Knowing that you can be replaced gives you the freedom to more fully enjoy your work.

Work (and dance) like nobody's watching

There is something very powerful in moving joyfully through a workplace. Walking and working as if no other being on earth can see you move. You can kick up your legs and swing your arms and celebrate just being alive. Working like no one is watching you gives you the freedom to really live and enjoy your work environment. Other people in your workplace are just like you. Other people get scared, confused, angry, embarrassed, upset, disappointed, treated unfairly, and surprised. What gives us the most power in any situation is the realization that hardly anyone ever wants you to fail and no one ever really cares if you do something crazy and fun. If you like to sing, then sing. If you like to dance, then dance. The only thing that matters here is that you are fully engaged and living your life full of as much passion as you can possibly handle. Just remember the age-old concept, "your freedom to swing your arms ends at the end of my nose." If you find passion in your workplace, embrace it to the fullest. You will be one of the lucky ones. This is not an original thought or idea (like so many other simple revolutionary acts), but it may be my very favorite one of them all. Nike says it all the time. "Just do it." Don't worry what other people think. Bon appetite.

Boldly try new ideas, methods, or things

I don't really care to eat fried chicken. Yet, I try to eat fried chicken at least once a year to make sure that I still don't like it. If I suddenly started liking it and didn't know I liked it, think how many opportunities that I would miss to eat fried chicken. In many ways, this is like trying new ideas, methods, or things in your workplace. You don't know what won't work until you try out the new idea, method, or thing. If it works, you have just reinvigorated your entire work group. If the new idea, method, or thing fails, you have collected important data about your attempt. Either way, you cannot lose. Don't assume just because something didn't work three years ago it will not work now. Think about consequences that surround doing new things, but don't think about them as being only two-valued (right or wrong, good and evil, black or white, country or western). Thinking about consequences allows a certain amount of freedom from risk to try new things. The only way to start a simple revolution in your workplace is to try a simple revolutionary act. No matter how you cut it, you are going to have to try something new. New ideas can often invigorate those around you. New methods cause you to view old problems in a new way. New things in your work environment make people look at the same old workplace with a new set of eyes.

Change a pattern of behavior

Everyday you perform your common workplace tasks in much the same way. Having a fixed routine is not all bad—in many ways, a fixed routine will make your life dependable, easier, and within your control, for a while. However, these patterns of behavior can be one of the primary reasons we wake up one morning and wonder where our life went. Patterns can cover huge gaps in our happiness and meaningfulness. Patterns can create the feeling of being trapped by our own lives. Try identifying patterns, figuring out why these patterns exist and what they do for us, and then changing them. Change your route to work. Change what you do everyday at the same time. Do things differently in the workplace. Get out of your own comfort zone—if even for a little bit of time. Changing patterns causes people to change the way they view the daily tasks that end up becoming our life. Do not allow yourself to miss a part of the excitement, the rush of adrenalin, that doing something new has on you and your career. Miss a train once and see what happens to your workplace. Always try and remember that time marches on whether you are at your desk at 7:07 a.m. every morning or not. Sometimes, it is quite appropriate to stop and smell the roses.

Hang out with people who challenge you to grow and be different

According to people who study the process of building and maintaining a sense of self-esteem, at least a quarter of the influences that effect the makeup of our sense of self-esteem come directly from the associations we have with other people. It is no secret to you that, in many ways, the way you feel about your workplace is directly related to the type of people who surround you at work. Much of how you feel about yourself comes from the type of people you surround yourself with. Knowing that you have few choices around the selection of your co-workers, peers, partners, customers, and staff, it really is revolutionary to ensure that you have surrounded yourself with people who move you forward. Find people who make you think new ideas, find people who rejuvenate and revitalize you. Find people who cause you to learn new things. Once you have found these people, become friends with them. Edward Hall, the father of non-verbal communication study, once told me that the only way to understand a new culture, to learn about the world around you, and to better grasp what factors make you behave the way you behave, is to make a friend. His assignments to college students in the universities where he taught were always the same, "during this semester you will have to make a friend." It is very important to actively choose to make friends with people who will demand you to be more or to grow. Just as you should not let your work act upon you, you should not rely solely on the universe to give you friendships. Hang out with people who challenge you.

Work with (or Hire) people smarter than you

Great managers hire even greater people. You know this because your manager hired you. Surround yourself with people who are one step ahead of you. Hire people in your office who will challenge you to be smarter, faster, and better. Create a staff that is willing to tell you the truth, because you tell them the truth. Then, get out of the way of these talented people. Allow them to ebb and flow knowing all along that there is a natural rhythm to the performance of work. Allow these people to make you proud. Create a space in your work environment where everything and everyone is allowed to be as smart and as innovative as they possibly can be. Provide all the tools needed to do the work and then provide the right tools that these people need to be creative. Move obstacles out of the way for your peers, co-workers, friends, partners, and customers. Be attuned to the needs of the group. Know that if you can gather information about potential hurdles, hazards, and pitfalls before these people get to them, you will have provided the exact environment that fosters success. Actively recruit people who you believe can make a difference in your programmatic and production needs, but will also be a shot in the arm to the sociological landscape of your group. When you figure out how important the people around you are to your own level of personal satisfaction, you begin to realize the importance of making and keeping high quality associations with other people.

*Look for people who do their jobs
extremely well and celebrate,
duplicate, and explore what it is
that makes them different*

It is extremely revolutionary to duplicate success. We, as a workplace society, are problem solvers. The way we do our work is to look for a problem, identify some potential solutions, and test some of the potential solutions to see which ones work best. Once we have gathered that information, we solve the problem. This is the classic problem-solving model. Francis Bacon called it the scientific method. We have grown very comfortable with this problem-solving method. In doing so, we have lost the ability to search for little moments of success, little pockets of good work. We must rekindle our ability to identify good work or good workers. Once we have these people identified, we must observe them and ask them the details of how and why they do the quality of work they do.

Be spontaneous

You are an interesting person. I can make such a claim because I have found most people are very interesting. You should act more interesting. By acting more interesting, I am urging you to behave in a less predictable way. Be spontaneous as a way of supporting a simple revolutionary act. Move a meeting. Surprise people around you. Do something clever and interesting and completely out of character. What is important in the act of being spontaneous is the very process of doing something without much warning, just for fun, and somewhat out of character. The event itself hardly matters. What matters is the spontaneity of the event. Be positively spontaneous, but not unpredictable. Be pleasantly spontaneous in behaviors that reward the positive actions of other people within your work environment. Just try to be fun and interesting to the people around you.

Surprise someone, somehow

Never pass up a chance to surprise a person in a positive way. There is something special about a surprise, the mixture of your excitement and the response of the person being surprised. It's a combination of not knowing what is happening balanced with disbelief that you have done anything to warrant such a treat from your co-workers. You can even surprise yourself by responding to a situation in a way that you would never expect yourself to respond. Surprise yourself, but also surprise other people with your decisions and responses to normal workplace events. Cover another person's shift one day. Send people home early. Sing the message on your voice mail. Bring the messiest snack food to work and then follow it up with a bucket and towels for cleaning up. Don't be afraid of how people will respond to you. The entire reason you are doing something surprising—your operational, tactical, and strategic goal—is to have people respond to you. About the only way you will be convinced to do something surprising is to do something surprising and monitor what happens to the way other people around you interact with you in your workplace. Remember, there is no experimental testing ground for simple revolutionary acts quite as good as your workplace.

Secretly do something good for a co-worker

Occasionally, when you really sense the time is right, pick a person you work with and do something special for that person. Buy them a soda, or pick up a client-job, or leave them an anonymous compliment on the feedback line. No fanfare, no credit, nobody ever has to know, but watch how this makes you feel about your work, your life, and your co-workers. This isn't a petty exercise. It is, however, an exercise in your skill of observing those who work around you and your ability to thoughtfully increase the quality of workplace relationships—for you and for them. Giving of yourself, secretly, is not an easy assignment, but it is a very important assignment for you and the way you feel about your workplace and the people you work with.

Take someone to lunch

There is much praise to be given about the joys of lunch. Lunch breaks up our day. Lunch nourishes our bodies, minds, and souls. Lunch is a great way for us to get away from the office, forget for a while about our desktops, and enjoy some personal time. Lunch has traditionally been a way for us to see and be seen, a place to close that big deal, and a very effective way to get to know the people we work with. We should celebrate lunch and understand that lunch is a great time to practice simple revolutionary acts. You don't have to spend a lot of money. Lunch doesn't have to be fancy. You can even pack an extra lunch and have a picnic. The importance of this simple suggestion is found in treating one of the people you work with to something that may seem special and unusual. Suddenly, you have created a person within your work group who feels, if even for a moment, special and recognized. This process will increase your ability to build and maintain relationships within your work environments. Try it and see what happens, but don't expect an invitation in return. This act is about giving of your self, unselfishly with no expectation of a returned favor, while building and maintaining relationships within your work group.

Sneak out and see a matinee with your co-workers

Seeing a movie in the afternoon seems like a luxury. Seeing a movie in the afternoon—on the clock, during work hours—doesn't seem like a luxury, it is a luxury. Let's face it: We need a bit of luxury every now and again. What a way to build a friendship and create a common story that your co-workers can tell their families around the dinner table. These activities, and others like it, help to build relationships by giving your co-workers, peers, partners, and customers a story that is unique, unusual, or different that people can use to differentiate between a common workplace and a workplace that is undergoing some simple revolutionary acts.

Bring ice cream bars* to a meeting that promises to be painful

...Or a meeting you are dreading, or will be boring, or one where you don't know the outcome. Do not be afraid to break some conventions in order to revitalize your co-workers, peers, customers, and friends. Bringing non-adult food to a meeting that promises extremely high levels of tension or boredom—or both—is to change the form of this specific workplace encounter. Try to lead your co-workers to a different response position and try to do that not by rhetoric or argument, but by changing the form of the meeting, the maturity level, or the environment. As odd as this sounds, every once in a while, try to bring down the level of maturity in this type of meeting. What happens to a meeting when you change the form or environment of that meeting is worth watching because the meeting is not usual, people engage with each other in different ways, and that will lead to different results. This simple revolutionary act also has far-reaching benefits. When you plan on changing the form of a meeting, you become naturally more excited about having the meeting. This excitement will cause you to engage in the planning, preparation, and facilitation of this event in a much different way—dare I say, a better and more excited way.

*And don't be limited to just ice cream for there are many great treats in this world.

Write a thank-you note every day

I know a handwritten note is a very personal and meaningful event for its recipient. I write at least one note a day to the people in my life. Writing a personal note to someone not only allows you to recognize the importance other people play in your life, but also helps you create, monitor, and maintain your connection to the peers, partners, customers, and co-workers that make up your work environment. Committing to writing personal notes causes you to actively seek people and processes that, in your opinion, are doing good things in your workplace. Then you reward these people by simply and beautifully recognizing their place in the workplace. The process of challenging yourself to find a target for your daily note will change the way you move, respond, and identify with your workplace. When you adapt your thinking to actively search for positive encounters within your workplace, guess what happens. You suddenly start finding positive encounters within your workplace. Thus, your note-writing obligation really becomes a way for you to make yourself change the way you think about your work. Why not use this simple revolutionary act to justify going to one of those stationery store and ordering personalized note cards? Having personalized note cards is classy, inpressive, and convenient.

Make Your Bed

A long time ago, I read one sentence that was tucked deep in an article titled something like "Insuring your Mental Health." This article contained an idea that revolutionized my life. One little line absolutely changed the way I lived. The article stated, "An unmade bed is a sign of poor mental health." I read that single line and thought to myself, "well hell, if that is all it takes to have good mental health, I will make my bed every morning." And I have promptly done just that. I have never, ever not made my bed in the morning, every morning for years and years. I now realize that making or not making your bed has very little to do with the state of your mental well-being. But I also know that one simple line in a magazine article made me a different person. Talk about the power of the press. I start my day, everyday, with a well-made bed and positive mental health. I also believe one well-placed line to some manager somewhere may just have the same effect.

After

This is just a sampling of some of the simple acts that can revolutionize the way you and your co-workers, peers, partners, friends, and customers feel about your workplace. There are many ways to revitalize and rejuvenate the people who work around you. No one answer is any better than any other answer. Not all of these simple revolutionary acts will work in all workplaces or all work cultures. Just as not all of these revolutionary acts are even appropriate to all workplaces. Some are much better than others for the place where you work.

Hopefully you have thought of some of your own simple revolutionary acts. I am even more hopeful that you have tried some of these simple revolutionary acts with your co-workers, friends, partners, peers, and customers. If you want to share these with others, I promise I will keep an ongoing list of really good ideas that are brought to the attention of the world. I also promise that I will also do my best to bring these new ideas to you. If you think of any simple revolutionary acts that you want to add to this list, drop me a line.

My address: Simple Revolutionary Acts

                            C/O Todd Conklin

                            P.O. Box 63

                            Santa Fe, New Mexico 87504

All of these acts are dictated by the contextual knowledge that you have experienced, learned, and carry with you about your workplace. You know what will work, what might work, and what may never work in your environment. Use the acts that you think will work best for your work environment. Don't use these contextual factors as an excuse for not taking risks. Risk, in most cases, is rewarded in our workplaces.

We live and work in high-stressed, fast-paced work environments. If meaningfulness and personal accomplishment account for anything, we have to make some changes in the way we see ourselves and the way we perceive our workplaces. The choice is simple. We can either do something or do nothing. Isn't doing something much better in the long run than doing nothing? Nothing is what we are doing right now, and it is getting us nowhere. As stress and uncertainty increase, often our ability to be risk-takers decreases. Either way, some change must take place or you and your co-workers will perform the most revolutionary act of all: You will leave.

About the Author

Todd Conklin has his Ph.D. in organizational communication and behavior and works as a manager at Los Alamos National Laboratory. Conklin works with groups internationally as an organizational development consultant, working mostly with programs that specialize in the detection of unusual behaviors in the workplace.

Being a national expert on unusual behavior pretty much fully-qualifies him to write about quality of work-life issues. Who else would be able to fully appreciate the goofy places where we work?

Todd Conklin loves to travel the world and when he isn't in some jungle in Southeast Asia you will find him laughing and riding his scooter through Santa Fe, New Mexico.

0-595-32065-1